LIVING WELL

SAFETY IN YOUR

NEIGHBORHOOD

by Lucia Raatma

THE CHILD'S WORLD®
CHANHASSEN, MINNESOTA

The Child's World

Published in the United States of America by The Child's World®
PO Box 326, Chanhassen, MN 55317-0326
800-599-READ
www.childsworld.com

Content Adviser:
Bridget Clementi,
Safe Kids Coordinator,
Children's Health
Education Center,
Milwaukee, Wisconsin

Photo Credits: Cover/frontispiece: Digital Vision/Punchstock; cover corner: Getty Images/ Photodisc. Interior: Corbis: 6, 8 (Rolf Bruderer), 12 (Gabe Palmer), 24 (Craig Lovell), 25 (Steve Chenn), 31 (Tom & Dee Ann McCarthy); Corbis Sygma: 13; Getty Images/The Image Bank: 7 (Kaz Chiba), 18 (Vicky Kasala Productions), 21 (Andy Caulfield); Getty Images/Photodisc/Ryan McVay: 14; Getty Images/Stone: 9 (Jeff Mermelstein), 15 (Lawrence Migdale), 17 (Peter Cade), 27 (Michael Busselle); PhotoEdit: 11 (Mary Kate Denny), 22 (Jonathan Nourok), 23 (David Young-Wolff); PictureQuest: 5 (Ron Chapple/Thinkstock), 16 (Creatas), 20 (Bob Llewellyn/ Image State-Pictor), 26 (Kevin Beebe/Index Stock Imagery).

The Child's World®: Mary Berendes, Publishing Director

Editorial Directions, Inc.: E. Russell Primm, Editorial Director; Katie Marsico, Line Editor; Matt Messbarger, Editorial Assistant; Susan Hindman, Copy Editor; Sarah E. De Capua, Proofreader; Katherine Trickle and Stephen Carl Wender, Fact Checkers; Tim Griffin/ IndexServ, Indexer; Cian Loughlin O'Day, Photo Researcher; Linda S. Koutris, Photo Selector

The Design Lab: Kathleen Petelinsek, Design; Kari Thornborough, Page Production

Library of Congress Cataloging-in-Publication Data
Raatma, Lucia.
    Safety in your neighborhood / by Lucia Raatma.
        v. cm. — (Living well)
    Includes bibliographical references and index.
    Contents: Who is that man?—Your home and neighborhood—Knowing your neighbors—
Strangers on your street—Someone's at your door—Keeping your neighborhood safe—Glossary—
Questions and answers about neighborhood safety—
Helping a friend learn about neighborhood safety—Did you know?—How to learn more about
neighborhood safety.
        ISBN 1-59296-240-8 (library bound : alk. paper)
        1. Crime prevention—United States—Juvenile literature. 2. Neighborhood—United States—
Juvenile literature. 3. Safety education—Juvenile literature. [1. Crime prevention. 2. Neighborhood.
3. Safety.] I. Title. II. Living well (Child's World (Firm))
    HV7431.R22 2005
    613.6'6—dc22   2003027214

TABLE OF CONTENTS

CHAPTER ONE

WHO IS THAT MAN?

Katie was staring out of her bedroom window. She was supposed to

be asleep, but the thunder had woken her up. It was dark and gloomy

as she watched the rain hitting the rooftops and sidewalks. Would it

ever let up?

She was about to leave the window and try to get back to sleep

when she saw something moving beyond her fence. The streetlights

helped her see that the figure was in the Doyles' yard, and it was

moving along the side of their house. As she looked closer, she saw

that it was a man she did not recognize. He was dressed all in black,

and he seemed to be trying to open each window. Maybe he knew that

the Doyles were away for the weekend. Just then, one of the windows

opened, and the man hopped onto the ledge and went into the house!

If you call 9-1-1 during an emergency, try to stay calm and carefully listen to the operator's instructions. She may ask you to stay on the phone until help arrives.

Katie went to wake up her parents. Her mom grabbed the

phone and dialed 9-1-1. When the operator answered, her mom

explained that a man was breaking into her neighbors' home. She

gave her name and address, as well as the Doyles' address. Soon they

heard sirens. Two police cars were racing up the street with their lights flashing. Then they pulled into the Doyles' driveway. The

man ran from the house, but police officers caught him and put him

in handcuffs. A bag he was carrying spilled to the ground.

The police do their best to stop break-ins and other crimes, but they can always use your help! If you see someone acting suspiciously in your neighborhood, tell a trusted adult right away or dial 9-1-1.

The police officers came to Katie's house to talk to her and her parents. They told Katie and her family that the man had tried to steal all of Mrs. Doyle's jewelry and some money, too. "It's good you made that call to 9-1-1," one officer said. "You did your neighbors a big favor."

CHAPTER TWO

YOUR HOME AND NEIGHBORHOOD

Your home is a special place. It is where you spend time with your family. You sleep there, and you do your homework there. You probably play games and watch movies there, too.

Your home is more than somewhere to live—it is a place where you feel safe and enjoy spending time with your family.

Your neighborhood is the area around your house or apartment. In many ways, it is your home, too. You spend time with friends there. And you probably play in the neighborhood park. You and your neighbors might have parties and cookouts together.

Your neighborhood should be a fun place for you and your friends to enjoy a game of basketball, a picnic, or a day at the park. By following a few simple rules, you can make it a safe place, too.

Because your neighborhood is an important place for you, you probably want to keep it safe.

One way to do this is to make sure

Accidents such as this one can occur if streetlights aren't working properly. Always tell an adult right away if you notice that these lights are out.

that all streetlights and traffic lights are working. If streetlights are out, then it is too dark at night. That can be **dangerous.** If traffic lights are broken, people could have car **accidents.** If you see these or other problems in your neighborhood, tell your parents or another adult who can help.

CHAPTER THREE

KNOWING YOUR NEIGHBORS

One important way to keep your neighborhood safe is to know

your neighbors. Really knowing them is more than just knowing

their first names or saying hi when you see one another outside.

Knowing your neighbors means knowing their full names, playing

with their kids and pets, spending time with them, and letting them

get to know you, too.

If you do not know your neighbors, talk to your parents about

ways to change that. You could have a new family over for dinner.

Or you could have a party and invite the whole block (see sidebar

on page 14). Don't try to make friends without talking to your

parents first, though. It is good to follow their advice about getting

to know the people in your neighborhood.

The better you know your neighbors, the safer you will be. You can look out for them if they have a problem. Even helping an older neighbor carry in her groceries is a way to keep your neighborhood safe. Your help keeps her from carrying too much and hurting herself. It also might prevent a stranger from trying to steal her purse while she has her hands full.

Helping an older neighbor with her groceries is a good way to make your area a friendlier and safer place.

Get to know neighbors of all ages. It is helpful to have a friend you can trust who lives close by.

When you know your neighbors, you benefit as well. That older neighbor might be able to help you with a school project. And if you are in trouble or need a safe place to go, it is nice to have neighbors to rely on.

If you know your neighbors well, you will realize when there is a stranger in your neighborhood. It may just be someone who has come to visit. Or it may be someone looking for a new home. But it may also be a person who is dangerous.

Knowing your neighbors is helpful during bad weather. If a **hurricane** is expected, you can help one another board up your homes and get to a safe place. Or if a **tornado** or another storm damages your neighborhood, you can help one another clean up afterward. Scary things are easier to deal with if you all work together.

Tornados can cause a great deal of damage, but you'll rebuild your area more quickly if you and your neighbors work together.

You can get to know your neighbors better by having a party. If your parents agree that it is a good idea, you can plan a party for your whole block or street. On a nice sunny day, you can set up tables outside and play games. All the families can bring food. You can even have music and dancing.

If you live in an apartment building, you could include everyone on your floor or the whole building. You could use a courtyard or a nearby park for the party.

Have your friends or family help you organize the event. Put up flyers or give out invitations. Pay special attention to people who have just moved in. They will appreciate being included.

CHAPTER FOUR

STRANGERS ON YOUR STREET

When you are in your neighborhood, you probably see strangers all the time. A stranger is someone you do not know well. The woman who brings your mail every day is familiar to you. But if you do not know her name or address, she is a stranger to you. People who repair telephone lines and cable boxes are

Perhaps you recognize the woman who delivers mail to your home every day, but she is still probably a stranger.

You don't need to be afraid of strangers such as the deliveryman. Most strangers are friendly people just like you, but it is still important to be cautious around them.

strangers. And so are people who make deliveries.

There is no reason to be afraid of these people. But you should also be aware that you do not know them well enough to trust them. If they ever ask you to get into their cars or try to come into your house without permission, yell as loudly as you can! Find an adult you trust, or get to a phone and call 9-1-1.

When you are walking or biking in your neighborhood, be aware of everything around you. Try to avoid shortcuts and alleys. It is always best to walk and bike in areas where other people are present. While you are out, you will see some strangers as well as some friends. A stranger might try to **lure** you by offering money or candy. If this happens, yell as loudly as

When biking through your neighborhood, pay attention to your surroundings and try to ride through areas where other people are present.

If you find yourself in trouble, a restaurant is a good place to go for help.

you can. You can yell, "This is not my mom!" or "This is not my

dad!" That will let other people know you are in trouble. You can

also run into the nearest public place, such as a store or restaurant.

People working there can help you or can call 9-1-1. Know the businesses in your neighborhood so you always have a safe place to go if you are in trouble.

Some strangers in your neighborhood might try to sell drugs to you or your friends. Ignore these strangers and keep moving, but try to remember what they look like. As soon as you are safely away from them, tell an adult or call 9-1-1. Do your best to give a good description of the people who approached you.

In some neighborhoods, dangerous groups can cause all kinds of trouble. These groups are called gangs. Some of these gangs are involved with drugs. Often gangs will ask people to pass tests before they are allowed to become members. These tests can be illegal and sometimes involve stealing something or even hurting someone. If you know of gangs in your neighborhood, talk to your parents about what you can all do to stop them.

CHAPTER FIVE

SOMEONE'S AT
YOUR DOOR

What do you do if someone knocks on your door or rings the doorbell? If either your parents or a babysitter is with you, ask what you should do. If you are home alone and are not expecting anyone, you should consider not answering the door at all. But if you know a friend or family member is coming to visit, you should follow some rules before opening the door.

The first thing is to ask who is there. If the

If you're home alone and the doorbell rings, consider not answering it at all if you're not expecting a visitor.

Before you let a police officer in, ask to see his badge through a window or peephole.

person is a friend or family member, it is OK to open the door.

If the person says he is a police officer, ask to see his badge

before you let him in. He can show his badge through a window

If you ask a stranger to come back later and she still won't go away, immediately call 9-1-1.

or **peephole.** If the person says she has a delivery, tell her to leave it at the door. But if she says she needs you to sign for it, tell her to come back another time. Never say that you are alone. Just say your parents are busy. If the person won't go away, call 9-1-1 and report the problem.

Sometimes you might feel sorry for someone at your door. Maybe it is kids selling candy for school. It may seem safe to open the door, but it might not be. Tell them to come back at a different time. Or the person at the door might say she has an **emergency** and needs to use your phone. Without opening the door, you can offer to call 9-1-1 for her.

It may seem impolite to refuse to open your door, but you are just staying safe. Sometimes strangers may try to trick you. They might want to get into your home to steal something or to hurt you.

Even if someone your age comes to the door, ask that person to come back later if he is a stranger.

CHAPTER SIX

KEEPING YOUR NEIGHBORHOOD SAFE

Most of the time, your neighborhood is probably a nice place. You might have a favorite park where you play. Or your best friend might live right next door. So you want your neighborhood to be safe.

The best rule is to keep your eyes open. If you see trouble, report it to an adult. Call 9-1-1 if you see a home on fire or if you see

You can help keep your neighborhood safe by staying alert and reporting any trouble to a trusted adult.

Your local hospital might be a good place to learn first aid.

someone breaking into a home. Learn first aid and other lifesaving

treatments at your local Red Cross office or hospital. Take the time

to help neighbors who may need you. If lights are broken or if the

playground is a mess, talk to your parents or other adults about getting

these problems fixed. Take on the **responsibility** of making your

neighborhood a safe place to live.

Neighborhood Watch

Neighborhood Watch is an organization that was formed to encourage people to work with police by watching for and reporting any suspicious activity in their neighborhoods. It is a way of helping the police—and you—keep your neighborhood safe. There are Neighborhood Watch groups all over the country, and they are made up of people such as you and your parents. Your city or town may have such a group. If so, contact them for more information.

Here are some things that Neighborhood Watch members notice and report:

- Cars that are abandoned
- People looking into windows or parked cars
- Strangers sitting in cars or stopping to talk to children
- Unusual noises
- Items being taken out of businesses that are closed or out of homes when the residents are not there
- Someone screaming or shouting for help
- Cars or trucks moving slowly down the street without lights on (at night) or with no apparent place to go
- Anyone being forced into a car
- **Graffiti** or other signs that might show if gangs are moving into an area

Glossary

accidents (AK-si-duhnts) Accidents are events that take place unexpectedly and often involve people being hurt.

dangerous (DAYN-jur-uhss) Something that is dangerous is likely to cause harm. It is not safe.

emergency (i-MUR-juhn-see) An emergency is a sudden and dangerous situation that requires immediate attention.

graffiti (gruh-FEE-tee) Graffiti is pictures or words written on surfaces such as the walls of buildings.

hurricane (HUR-uh-kane) A hurricane is a violent storm with strong winds. Hurricanes start in the Caribbean Sea or part of the Atlantic Ocean and sometimes move north toward the United States.

lure (LOOR) To lure someone is to lead that person into danger.

peephole (PEEP-hohl) A peephole is a hole or opening you can peek through to see to the other side. Peepholes are often found on front doors.

responsibility (ri-spon-suh-BIL-uh-tee) A responsibility is a duty or a job.

tornado (tor-NAY-doh) A tornado is a huge, whirling column of air that is shaped like a funnel. Its strong winds can destroy everything in its path.

Questions and Answers about Neighborhood Safety

I saw a couple of men trying to get into my neighbor's house. It's none of my business, right? Wrong! Looking out for your neighborhood is everyone's business. If you suspect that someone is trying to break into a house, call 9-1-1. Or, at least call the neighbor to check on him.

When my friends and I were walking home, a couple of older kids offered us something. We couldn't tell what it was, but they said we'd have a good time. We ignored them—was that OK? Absolutely. And you should report them, too. What they were offering you was probably drugs, and you should steer clear of them.

The stop sign on my street was knocked down. Is there anything I can do? Sure. Call your local police department right away and report the problem. Without that stop sign, people could have car accidents.

Helping a Friend Learn about Neighborhood Safety

▸ Ask your friend to take a first aid course with you. That way, you can help each other learn and will be ready to help others who might need you.

▸ Tell your friend how you have tried to get to know your neighbors. Encourage her to do the same thing.

▸ Stick together. You and your friend can make plans to always bike and walk together. Avoid shortcuts and deserted alleys. Being together will make you feel safer in your neighborhood.

Did You Know?

▸ One great way to keep your neighborhood safe is for you and your neighbors to work with the police to prevent crimes from happening.

▸ Gangs can ruin the neighborhood for everyone. If you know of a gang, or if you are approached to join one, it is best to talk to an adult you trust right away.

▸ Neighborhoods are everywhere—from big cities to tiny towns and everywhere in between!

How to Learn More about Neighborhood Safety

At the Library

Chaiet, Donna, and Francine Russell. *The Safe Zone: A Kid's Guide to Personal Safety.* New York: Beech Tree, 1998.

Girard, Linda Walvoord. *Who Is a Stranger and What Should I Do?* Morton Grove, Ill.: Albert Whitman, 1985.

Pellegrino, Marjorie White. *My Grandma's the Mayor: A Story for Children about Community Spirit and Pride.* Washington, D.C.: Magination, 1999.

Sanders, Pete. *Personal Safety.* Brookfield, Conn.: Millbrook Press, 1998.

On the Web

Visit our home page for lots of links about neighborhood safety:
http://www.childsworld.com/links.html

Note to Parents, Teachers, and Librarians: We routinely verify our Web links to make sure they're safe, active sites—so encourage your readers to check them out!

Through the Mail or by Phone

American Red Cross National Headquarters
431 18th Street NW
Washington, DC 20006
202/303-4498

Federal Bureau of Investigation
Crimes against Children Program
935 Pennsylvania Avenue NW
Room 11163
Washington, DC 20535
202/324-3666

National Crime Prevention Council
1000 Connecticut Avenue NW
13th floor
Washington, DC 20036
202/466-6272

National Neighborhood Watch Institute
PO Box 4208
Sante Fe Springs, CA 90670
888/669-4872

National SAFE KIDS Campaign
1301 Pennsylvania Avenue NW
Suite 100
Washington, DC 20004
202/662-0600

Index

About the Author

Lucia Raatma received her bachelor's degree in English literature from the University of South Carolina and her master's degree in cinema studies from New York University. She has written a wide range of books for young people. When she is not researching or writing, she enjoys going to movies, practicing yoga, and spending time with her family. She lives in New York.